Rock Pool Animals

Siân Smith

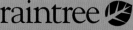
raintree
a Capstone company — publishers for children

Raintree is an imprint of Capstone Global Library Limited, a company incorporated in England and Wales having its registered office at 7 Pilgrim Street, London, EC4V 6LB – Registered company number: 6695582

www.raintreepublishers.co.uk
myorders@raintreepublishers.co.uk

Text © Capstone Global Library Limited 2015
First published in hardback in 2014
Paperback edition first published in 2015
The moral rights of the proprietor have been asserted.

Edited by Sian Smith and Diyan Leake
Designed by Marcus Bell
Picture research by Tracy Cummins
Production by Helen McCreath
Originated by Capstone Global Library Ltd
Printed and bound in China

ISBN 978 1 406 28069 2 (hardback)
18 17 16 15 14
10 9 8 7 6 5 4 3 2 1

ISBN 978 1 406 28076 0 (paperback)
19 18 17 16 15
10 9 8 7 6 5 4 3 2 1

British Library Cataloguing in Publication Data
Smith, Sian.
Rock pool animals. -- (Animal in their habitats)
A full catalogue record for this book is available from the British Library.

Acknowledgements
We would like to thank the following for permission to reproduce photographs: Getty Images pp. 4 (Ed Reschke), 5, 15 (Paul Kay), 6 (Reinhard Dirscherl), 8 (Franco Banfi), 13 (Hans Leijnse/ Foto Natura); Shutterstock pp. 7 (Joao Pedro Silva), 9 (Lynsey Allan), 10 (Matthew Gough), 20a (Semmick Photo), 20b (Kuttelvaserova Stuchelova), 20c (RaduTo), 20d (Moises Fernandez Acosta), 21 (Vincent Louis); Superstock pp. 11, 14, 22b (FLPA), 12 (Animals Animals), 16, 22a (NHPA), 17 (Fotosearch), 18 (Marevision / age fotostock), 19 (NaturePL).

Cover photograph of a Sally Lightfoot crab (*Grapsus grapsus*) foraging in a tidal pool, reproduced with permission of National Geographic Creative (JAMES FORTE).

Back cover photograph reproduced with permission of Superstock (Marevision / age fotostock).

We would like to thank Michael Bright for his invaluable help in the preparation of this book.

Every effort has been made to contact copyright holders of material reproduced in this book. Any omissions will be rectified in subsequent printings if notice is given to the publisher.

Contents

Animals in a rock pool

Come and see the starfish.

Come and see the blenny fish.

Come and see the anemone.

Come and see the goby fish.

Come and see the spider crab.

Come and see the hermit crab.

mussel

Come and see the mussel.

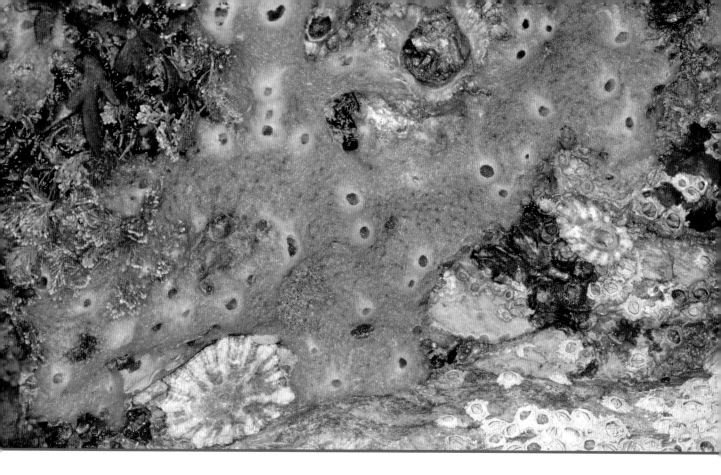

Come and see the sponge.

barnacle

Come and see the barnacle.

Come and see the snail.

limpet

Come and see the limpet.

Come and see the prawn.

Come and see the gunnel.

Come and see the cuttlefish.

Come and see the lobster.

Come and see the sea slug.

Living in a rock pool

seaweed

snowdrop

strawberry

You can find rock pools on a beach. They are filled with water from the sea.

Which plant can you find in a rock pool?

Answer: seaweed

What am I?

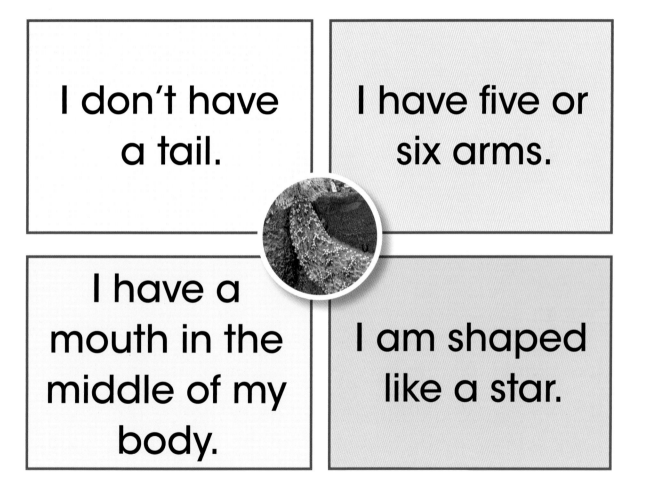

I don't have a tail.

I have five or six arms.

I have a mouth in the middle of my body.

I am shaped like a star.

Picture glossary

 gunnel

sponge

Index

Notes for teachers and parents

Before reading

Tuning in: Talk about what a rock pool is. What happens when the tide comes in? What happens when the tide goes out?

After reading

Recall and reflection: Why do many rock pool animals (mussels, anemones, limpets, barnacles) cling to the rocks?

Sentence knowledge: Help the child to count the number of words in each sentence.

Word knowledge (phonics): Encourage the child to point at the word *and* on any page. Sound out the phonemes in the word: *a-n-d*. Ask the child to sound out each letter as they point at it and then blend the sounds together to make the word *and*.

Word recognition: Challenge the child to race you to point at the word *come* on any page.

Rounding off

Say the tongue-twister:
She sells sea shells on the sea shore.
The shells that she sells are sea shells, I'm sure.

Word coverage

Topic words
anemone
barnacle
blenny fish
cuttlefish
goby fish
gunnel
hermit crab
limpet
lobster
mussel
octopus
prawn
sea
sea slug
snail
spider crab
sponge
starfish

High-frequency words
a
and
come
in
see
the

Sentence stem
Come and see the _____.

Ask children to read these words:

fish	p. 6
crab	p. 8
limpet	p. 14
lobster	p. 18
slug	p. 19